IN RECITAL®
WITH *Timeless Hymns*
(IN A CONTEMPORARY SETTING)

ABOUT THE SERIES • A NOTE TO THE TEACHER

In Recital® with Timeless Hymns is devoted to everlasting hymns that have been sung and heard throughout many generations. The outstanding arrangers of this series have created engaging arrangements of these hymns, which have been carefully leveled to ensure success. We know that to motivate, the teacher must challenge the student with attainable goals. This series makes that possible while also providing peaceful and joyous musical settings for your students. You will find favorites that are easy to sing along with, as well as recital-style arrangements. This series complements other FJH publications, and will help you plan student performances throughout the years. The books include CDs with complete performances designed to assist with performance preparation as well as for pure listening pleasure. Throughout this series you will find interesting background information for the hymns by Lyndell Leatherman.

Use the enclosed CD as a teaching and motivational tool. For a guide to listening to the CD, turn to page 48.

Production: Frank J. Hackinson
Production Coordinators: Joyce Loke and Satish Bhakta
Cover Design: Terpstra Design, San Francisco, CA
Cover Illustration: Keith Alexander
Engraving: Tempo Music Press, Inc.
Printer: Tempo Music Press, Inc.

ISBN-13: 978-1-56939-925-5

ORGANIZATION OF THE SERIES
IN RECITAL® WITH TIMELESS HYMNS

T he series is carefully leveled into the following six categories: Early Elementary, Elementary, Late Elementary, Early Intermediate, Intermediate, and Late Intermediate. Each of the works has been selected for its artistic as well as its pedagogical merit.

Book Five — Intermediate, reinforces the following concepts:

■ Triplet and sixteenth-note patterns are used, as well as dotted-rhythmic patterns and syncopated rhythms.

■ Students play scale passages and octaves.

■ Chords and their inversions are reinforced.

■ Students play pieces with simple and compound meters.

■ A mixture of keys strengthen the student's command of the piano.

Abide With Me and *Shall We Gather at the River* were composed as equal-part duets. The rest of the selections are solo.

TABLE OF CONTENTS

FJH2146

ABOUT THE PIECES AND COMPOSERS

It Is Well with My Soul

In 1870, life was good for Horatio Spafford, a successful lawyer and businessman living in Chicago with his wife Anna and four daughters. But some time after the great Chicago fire of 1871, he took his family to New York and put them on the S.S. Ville du Havre, the largest passenger ship of its day, with a promise to join them in Paris. Tragically, in the early morning darkness of November 22, 1873, as it was off the coast of Newfoundland, the ship was accidently rammed broadside by another ship, sinking in twelve minutes. All four girls perished but not Anna, who was one of only twenty-two who survived (from a passenger list of 500). After being rescued she was transferred to a ship bound for Cardiff, Wales. For two weeks, the overcrowded, under-stocked ship fought North Atlantic storms before reaching land. Upon arrival, Anna sent a two-word message via cable to her husband: "saved alone." Immediately Horatio traveled to the East Coast and boarded a ship for Wales. Tracing the same route taken by the Ville du Havre, the captain notified Spafford as they passed over the location of the disaster. Overcome with his loss, yet refusing to lose faith, he went back to his cabin where he began to pour out his feelings on paper. Three years later the resulting poem was set to music by the well-known Philip P. Bliss, and the hymn has since become a favorite around the world.

Swing Low, Sweet Chariot

In the Bible we are told that the prophet Elijah didn't die when his time on earth was done. Instead a chariot of fire came down from the sky, and he stepped in and rode it to heaven. *Swing Low, Sweet Chariot* was inspired by this Bible story and then embellished as it passed from generation to generation. Again, as in many other hymns and spirituals, the Jordan River is a symbol of the boundary between this life and the next. The song may also have contained coded messages about the Underground Railroad, a network of "safe houses" that helped slaves escape into northern states or Canada. Read the lyrics and notice that they could either refer to heaven or freedom in the North.

Christ the Lord Is Risen Today

Charles Wesley (1707-1788) and his brother John (1703-1791) both trained for ministry at Oxford University. Some other students jokingly called them "methodists" because of the strict schedule (or method) of religious exercises and study habits that they developed. After a short unsuccessful trip as missionaries to the American Colonies, they returned home to England discouraged. But during the sea voyage back to England, spiritual seeds were planted in their hearts as they watched a group of

ABOUT THE PIECES AND COMPOSERS

Moravians experiencing amazing peace during a violent storm that threatened to sink their ship. Soon the brothers experienced spiritual rebirth, and the rest is history, with John's preaching and Charles' hymn writing (over 6,500 hymn texts written in his lifetime!) starting a great revival that swept across England and became the foundation of the Methodist denomination.

Christ the Lord Is Risen Today was originally eleven stanzas long, with no alleluias at the end of the phrases. No one knows who wrote this tune, which had first appeared in *Lyra Davidica*, a hymnal published in 1708 in London. The text and tune were first combined in the *Foundery Collection*, edited in 1742 by John Wesley, at which time the alleluias were added.

Peace Like a River

When you look at a large river from a distance, it looks so peaceful as it winds through the countryside. There may be lots of things happening down below—from whirlpools to carnivorous creatures to jagged obstacles that can tear open the hull of a boat—but on the surface all seems well. The anonymous composer of this song felt that life could be this way: no matter what we are dealing with below the surface, we can have a peaceful, easy feeling when we are one with our Creator.

How Firm a Foundation

In 1787, an English minister named John Rippon compiled a hymnal with the less-than-catchy title, *A Selection of Hymns*. Included in the collection was a text titled *How Firm a Foundation, Ye Saints of the Lord*, with its shy author identified only as "K". That text has since appeared in nearly every major hymnal to this present day.

The first stanza reminds Christians that the Bible is the foundation for their faith. The remaining stanzas are enclosed in quotation marks, indicating that they are promises taken directly from scripture, although rewritten as poems. For example, stanza 2 comes from Isaiah 41:10 (KJV): "Fear thou not, for I am with thee; be not dismayed, for I am thy God. I will strengthen thee, yea, I will help thee. Yea, I will uphold thee with the right hand of my righteousness."

The tune is also anonymous, first appearing in Caldwell's *Union Harmony*, published in the United States in 1837.

for Christine Wise

It Is Well with My Soul

Music by Philip P. Bliss
Lyrics by Horatio G. Spafford
arr. Edwin McLean

7

FJH2146

8

Swing Low, Sweet Chariot

African-American Spiritual
arr. Nancy Lau

FJH2146

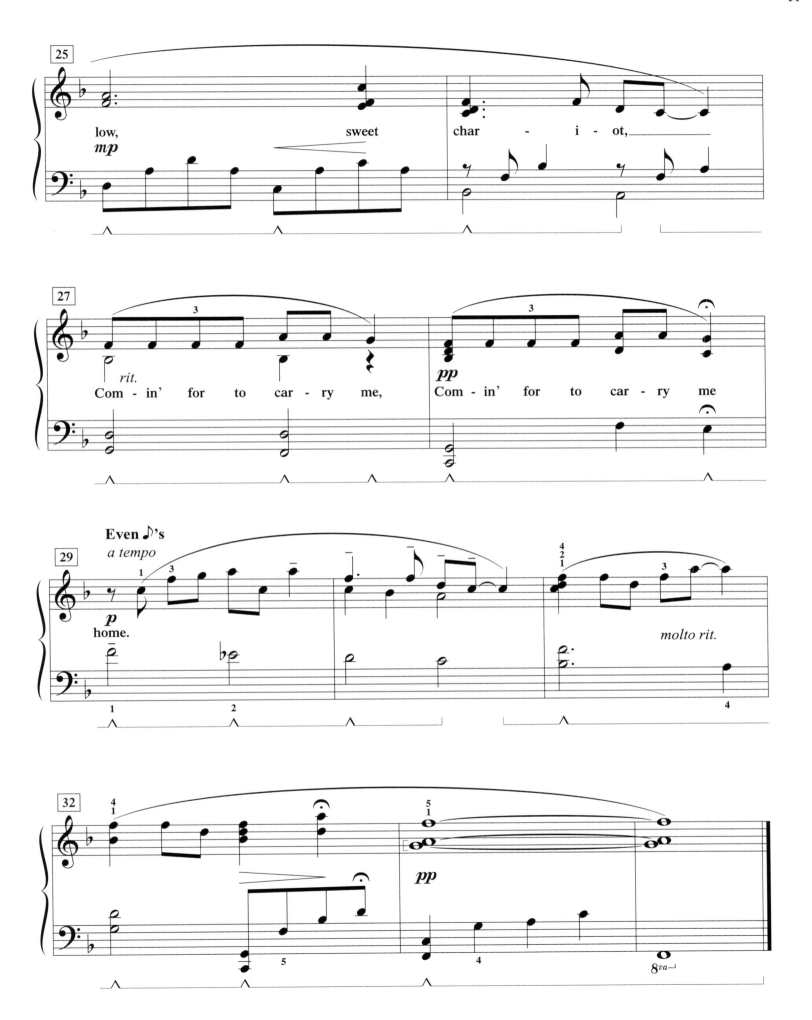

Christ the Lord Is Risen Today

Music from *Lyra Davidica*
Lyrics by Charles Wesley
arr. Edwin McLean

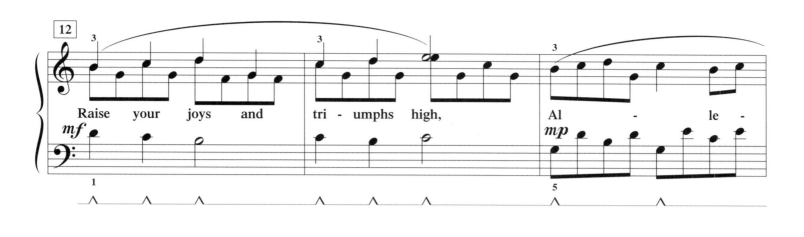

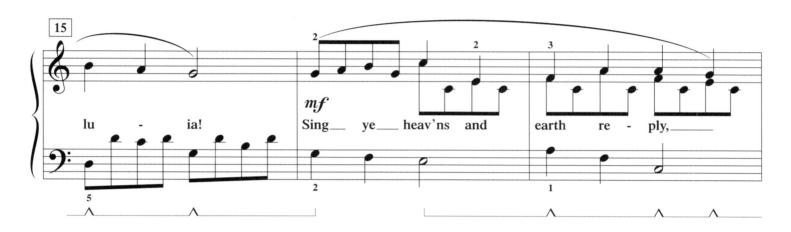

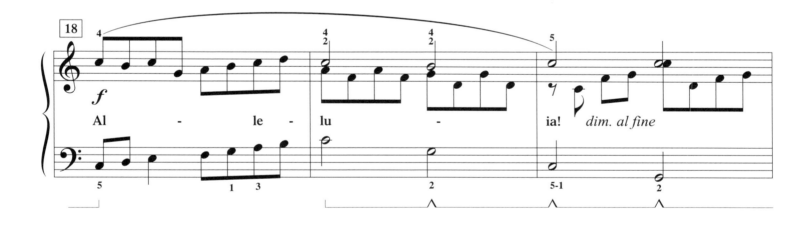

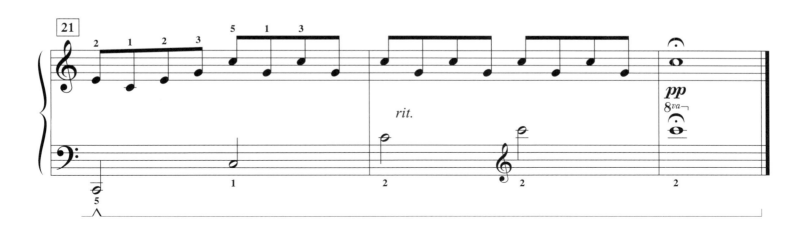

Peace Like a River

Traditional
arr. Edwin McLean

with light pedal

I've got peace like a river,
I've got peace like a river,
I've got peace like a river in my soul;
I've got peace like a river,
I've got peace like a river,
I've got peace like a river in my soul.

FJH2146

How Firm a Foundation

Music: Traditional American Melody
Lyrics from John Rippon's *Selection of Hymns*
arr. Nancy Lau

19

FJH2146

Abide With Me
Secondo

Music by William H. Monk
Lyrics by Henry F. Lyte
arr. Nancy Lau

FJH2146

Abide With Me
Primo

Music by William H. Monk
Lyrics by Henry F. Lyte
arr. Nancy Lau

FJH2146

Secondo

Joshua Fought the Battle of Jericho

African-American Spiritual
arr. Valerie Roth Roubos

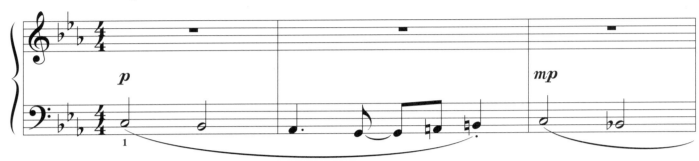

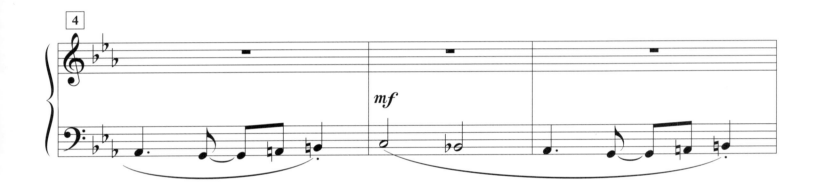

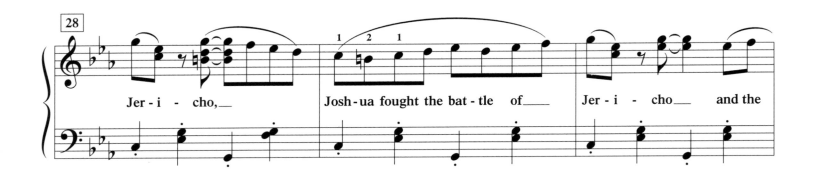

Jer - i - cho,__ Josh-ua fought the bat - tle of__ Jer - i - cho__ and the

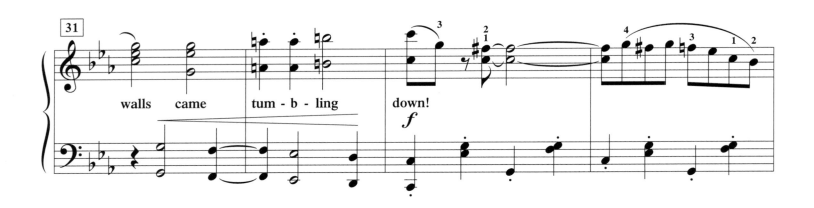

walls came tum - b - ling down!

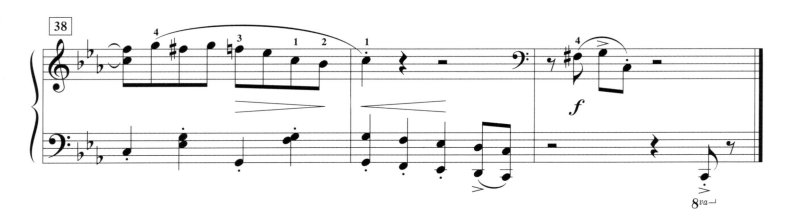

The Old Rugged Cross

George Bennard
arr. Edwin McLean

FJH2146

28

2. Oh, that old rugged cross, so despised by the world,
   Has a wondrous attraction for me;
   For the dear Lamb of God, left His glory above
   To bear it on dark Calvary.
   So I'll cherish the old rugged cross,
   Till my trophies at last I lay down;
   I will cling to the old rugged cross,
   And exchange it someday for a crown.

What Wondrous Love Is This

Music from William Walker's *Southern Harmony*
Lyrics: Traditional American
arr. Kevin Olson

He's Got the Whole World in His Hands

Spiritual
arr. Robert Schultz

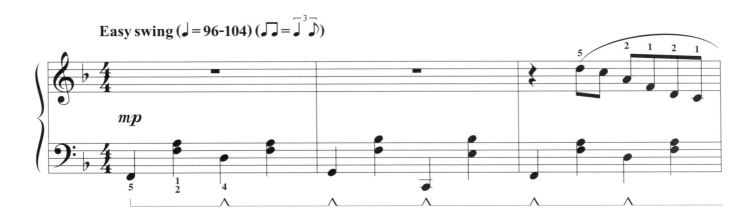

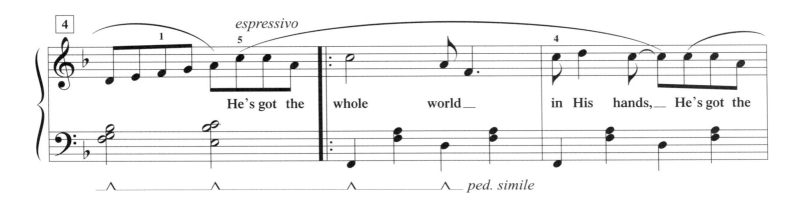

FJH2146

34

He's got the whole world

in His hands,_ He's got the whole_ world_ in His hands,_ He's got the

whole world_ in His hands,_ He's got the whole world in His

hands.

He's (got) the

Come, Thou Fount of Every Blessing

Music from John Wyeth's *Repository of Sacred Music, Part Second*
Lyrics by Robert Robinson
arr. Robert Schultz

38

FJH2146

Come, Thou Fount of every blessing,
Tune my heart to sing Thy grace;
Streams of mercy, never ceasing,
Call for songs of loudest praise.
Teach me some melodious sonnet,
Sung by flaming tongues above.
Praise the mount! I'm fixed upon it,
Mount of Thy redeeming love.

Shall We Gather at the River
Secondo

Robert Lowry
arr. Valerie Roth Roubos

Shall We Gather at the River
Primo

Robert Lowry
arr. Valerie Roth Roubos

FJH2146

Secondo

ABOUT THE PIECES AND COMPOSERS

Abide With Me

Henry Francis Lyte was born in Kelso, Ireland in 1793. After attending college and seminary, he became a minister in Ireland and England. His church at Brixham-on-Sea, England, was mainly attended by sailors and fishermen and their families. While still quite young, Pastor Lyte came down with tuberculosis, and for much of the rest of his life he felt ill. But he continued pastoring his congregation for almost twenty-five years, and his people loved him dearly. Finally, his doctor convinced him that moving to the drier, warmer climate of Italy was his only chance of survival. On the Sunday afternoon after he preached his last sermon, Lyte wrote this farewell hymn to his beloved church. Fourteen years later a music editor, William H. Monk, wrote a tune for Lyte's poem and included the resulting hymn in a new collection of songs: *Hymns Ancient and Modern*. Since then the hymn has been a favorite of millions of people around the world.

Joshua Fought the Battle of Jericho

One of the more interesting stories of the Old Testament involves a man named Joshua, a walled city, and a long hike. The Israelites had been commanded by God to drive away the wicked Canaanites who lived around them. But the Canaanite city of Jericho was too fortified to conquer. So God told the Israelites to march around the city six days in a row, and then on the seventh day to march around the city seven times. When they had all finished their seventh lap on the seventh day, the priests blew trumpets and the people all shouted, and the walls of Jericho crumbled, allowing the Israelites to overrun and conquer the city.

That story inspired this African-American spiritual, but the song went on to have coded meanings related to the Underground Railroad and the slaves' yearning for freedom. Its lively melody and rhythm also provided energy and inspiration as the slaves worked in the hot sun. The song has since been recorded by hundreds of singers, including Elvis Presley and Mahalia Jackson.

The Old Rugged Cross

Rev. George Bennard (1873-1958), from Albion, Michigan, began his ministry in the Salvation Army and later switched his membership to the Methodist Episcopal Church, where he served as a well-loved evangelist for many years. He is remembered today for one hymn—*The Old Rugged Cross*—which talks about the main symbol of Christianity, the cross, upon which Jesus of Nazareth was crucified.

This simple hymn quickly became one of the most published and recorded songs ever—including sacred and secular—with early boosts from people like Roy Rogers (the "singing cowboy") and Pat Boone.

ABOUT THE PIECES AND COMPOSERS

What Wondrous Love Is This

What Wondrous Love Is This is a very old American song, author unknown, which was passed along from singer to singer for many years. It was first captured on paper in 1835, when it appeared in a collection of hymns called *Southern Harmony*. The melody sounds cool and mysterious because it's in the Dorian mode, a scale that is neither major nor minor. You can make up other interesting Dorian melodies by improvising from D to D without using any black keys.

He's Got the Whole World in His Hands

No one knows for sure where this joyous song originated. Like other spirituals, it may have been improvised by African-American slaves to ease the boredom of their long hours of work. Or it may have been a part of their secret church services. Some people think that it was actually written by a Cherokee Native-American named Obie Phillis while he served as a soldier during World War II. In the 1950s it was recorded many times—by Mahalia Jackson, a gospel and soul singer; Marian Anderson, an opera star; and Perry Como, a "crooner."

Come, Thou Fount of Every Blessing

As a youth in London, Robert Robinson (1735-1790) was, by all accounts, destined for failure. Fatherless, he had joined a gang of troublemakers who roamed the streets. One night in 1752 their "agenda" included heckling a famous preacher, George Whitefield, who was speaking nearby. However, as the evangelist preached from the words of John the Baptist in Matthew 3:7: "O generation of snakes, who has warned you to flee from the judgment to come?" Robinson was reminded of his wickedness. That night he decided to turn his life around.

Six years later, Robinson—now a pastor himself—wrote *Come, Thou Fount of Every Blessing* for the service of Pentecost at his church. A dizzying mixture of metaphors, it is quite possibly the only hymn to ever speak of raising an "Ebenezer"! (According to I Samuel 7:12, this was the name given to a stone monument commemorating God's deliverance of His people, meaning literally, "stone of help.") Fifty-five years later, the text was combined with the anonymous early American tune that is most commonly associated with the hymn today.

Shall We Gather at the River

Robert Lowry (1826-1899) was born in Philadelphia, Pennsylvania. He attended the University of Lewisburg (later renamed Bucknell University), and then for a while taught literature there. After being ordained as a Baptist minister, he pastored churches in Pennsylvania, New York, and New Jersey. Along the way he wrote approximately 500 hymn texts or tunes. Although he had no formal training in music composition, he had an amazing ability to write memorable songs such as *Shall We Gather at the River*.

46

ABOUT THE ARRANGERS

Nancy Lau

Nancy Lau (pronounced "Law") has often been told that her music sounds very lyrical and natural. She discovered her love and talent for music early in life. Born with perfect pitch, by age four Nancy was able to play nursery rhymes on the piano by ear. She was soon coming up with her own arrangements of songs and was able to copy any music that she heard.

An active composer, arranger, and piano teacher, Nancy studied music composition with Dr. Norman Weston and piano pedagogy with Nakyong Chai at Saddleback College in Orange County, California. In addition to writing for piano, she has composed for solo voice and chamber ensemble, and has written many choral works. Her compositions have won numerous awards. Nancy maintains a full piano studio, where her emphasis is on keeping music enjoyable and exciting. She believes that students must feel nurtured and accepted, and strives to generate in her piano lessons a joyful experience and positive memory.

Edwin McLean

Edwin McLean is a composer living in Chapel Hill, North Carolina. He is a graduate of the Yale School of Music, where he studied with Krzysztof Penderecki and Jacob Druckman. He also holds a master's degree in music theory and a bachelor's degree in piano performance from the University of Colorado.

Mr. McLean has authored over 200 publications for The FJH Music Company, ranging from *The FJH Classic Music Dictionary* to original works for pianists from beginner to advanced. His highly-acclaimed works for harpsichord have been performed internationally and are available on the Miami Bach Society recording, *Edwin McLean: Sonatas for 1, 2, and 3 Harpsichords*. His 2011 solo jazz piano album *Don't Say Goodbye* (CD1043) includes many of his advanced works for piano published by FJH.

Edwin McLean began his career as a professional arranger. Currently, he is senior editor for The FJH Music Company Inc.

Kevin Olson

Kevin Olson is an active pianist, composer, and member of the piano faculty at Utah State University, where he teaches piano literature, pedagogy, and accompanying courses. In addition to his collegiate teaching responsibilities, Kevin directs the Utah State Youth Conservatory, which provides weekly group and private piano instruction to more than 200 pre-college community students. The National Association of Schools of Music has recently recognized the Conservatory as a model for pre-college piano instruction programs. Before teaching at Utah State, he was on the faculty at Elmhurst College near Chicago and Humboldt State University in northern California.

A native of Utah, Kevin began composing at age five. When he was twelve, his composition, *An American Trainride*, received the Overall First Prize at the 1983 National PTA Convention at Albuquerque, New Mexico. Since then he has been a Composer in Residence at the National Conference on Piano Pedagogy, and has written music commissioned and performed by groups such as the American Piano Quartet, Chicago a cappella, the Rich Matteson Jazz Festival, and several piano teacher associations around the country.

Kevin maintains a large piano studio, teaching students of a variety of ages and abilities. Many of the needs of his own piano students have inspired more than 100 books and solos published by the FJH Music Company, which he joined as a writer in 1994.

ABOUT THE ARRANGERS

Valerie Roth Roubos

Valerie Roth Roubos earned degrees in music theory, composition, and flute performance from the University of Wyoming. Ms. Roubos maintains a studio in her home in Spokane, Washington, where she teaches flute, piano, and composition.

Active as a performer, adjudicator, lecturer, and accompanist, Ms. Roubos has lectured and taught master classes at the Washington State Music Teachers Conference, Holy Names Music Camp, and the Spokane and Tri-Cities chapters of Washington State Music Teachers Association. She has played an active role in the Spokane Music Teachers Association and WSMTA.

In 2001, the South Dakota Music Teachers Association selected Ms. Roubos as Composer of the Year, and with MTNA commissioned her to write *An American Portrait: Scenes from the Great Plains*, published by The FJH Music Company Inc. Ms. Roubos was chosen to be the 2004–2005 composer-in-residence at Washington State University. In 2006, WSMTA selected her as Composer of the Year. Ms. Roubos' teaching philosophy and compositions reflect her belief that all students, from elementary to advanced, are capable of musical playing that incorporates sensitivity and expression. Her compositions represent a variety of musical styles, including sacred, choral, and educational piano works.

Robert Schultz

Robert Schultz, composer, arranger, and editor, has achieved international fame during his career in the music publishing industry. The Schultz Piano Library, established in 1980, has included more than 500 publications of classical works, popular arrangements, and Schultz's original compositions in editions for pianists of every level from the beginner through the concert artist. In addition to his extensive library of published piano works, Schultz's output includes original orchestral works, chamber music, works for solo instruments, and vocal music.

Schultz has presented his published editions at workshops, clinics, and convention showcases throughout the United States and Canada. He is a long-standing member of ASCAP and has served as president of the Miami Music Teachers Association. Mr. Schultz's original piano compositions and transcriptions are featured on the compact disc recordings *Visions of Dunbar* and *Tina Faigen Plays Piano Transcriptions*, released on the ACA Digital label and available worldwide. His published original works for concert artists are noted in Maurice Hinson's *Guide to the Pianist's Repertoire, Third Edition*. He currently devotes his full time to composing and arranging. In-depth information about Robert Schultz and The Schultz Piano Library is available at the Website www.schultzmusic.com.

USING THE CD

A great way to prepare for your recitals is to listen to the CD.

Enjoy listening to these wonderful pieces anywhere anytime! Listen to them casually (as background music) and attentively. After you have listened to the CD you might discuss interpretation with your teacher and follow along with your score as you listen.

HYMN PERFORMANCES

Hymns	Where Played	Date	Special Memory of the Event
It Is Well with My Soul			
Swing Low, Sweet Chariot			
Christ the Lord Is Risen Today			
Peace Like a River			
How Firm a Foundation			
Abide With Me			
Joshua Fought the Battle of Jericho			
The Old Rugged Cross			
What Wondrous Love Is This			
He's Got the Whole World in His Hands			
Come, Thou Fount of Every Blessing			
Shall We Gather at the River			